45 HEALTHY WAYS TO GET OUT DEPRESSION

Copywrite

TABLE OF CONTENTS

INTRODUCTION

Navigating life's challenges can be daunting, but there are ways to safeguard your mental health. Prioritize regular exercise, balanced nutrition, and sufficient sleep to nurture physical well-being. Cultivate supportive relationships and seek social connections to combat feelings of loneliness. Manage stress through mindfulness and relaxation techniques. Set achievable goals and practice self-compassion. Engage in activities that bring joy and purpose. Should persistent feelings of sadness arise, don't hesitate to seek professional guidance. By prioritizing self-care and seeking support when needed, you can build resilience and reduce the risk of depression.

Getting out of depression can be a challenging journey, but it's entirely possible with the right support, strategies, and mindset. Here's an introduction to some steps you can take:

Acknowledge Your Feelings: Recognize that it's okay to feel the way you do. Depression is a common and treatable condition, and acknowledging your emotions is the first step toward healing.

Seek Professional Help: Consider reaching out to a therapist, counselor, or psychiatrist who can provide you with guidance, support, and appropriate treatment options. Therapy can help you explore the root causes of your depression and develop coping strategies.

Build a Support System: Surround yourself with supportive friends, family members, or support groups who can offer encouragement, understanding, and a listening ear. Connecting with others who have experienced similar struggles can help you feel less alone.

Practice Self-Care: Prioritize self-care activities that promote physical, emotional, and mental well-being. This could include getting regular exercise, maintaining a healthy diet, practicing relaxation techniques such as mindfulness or meditation, and ensuring you get enough sleep.

Set Realistic Goals: Break tasks into smaller, manageable steps and set realistic goals for yourself. Celebrate your achievements, no matter how small, as each step forward is a victory in overcoming depression.

Challenge Negative Thoughts: Pay attention to negative thought patterns and challenge them with evidence-based reasoning. Cognitive-behavioral therapy (CBT) techniques can help you identify and reframe negative thoughts more positively.

Engage in Activities You Enjoy: Find activities that bring you joy, fulfillment, and a sense of accomplishment. Whether it's pursuing a hobby, spending time in nature, or volunteering, engaging in activities that bring you pleasure can help lift your mood.

Limit Stress: Identify sources of stress in your life and take steps to minimize or manage them. Practice time management, assertiveness, and boundary-setting to reduce overwhelm and maintain balance.

Stay Patient and Persistent: Recovery from depression takes time, and setbacks are a normal part of the process. Be patient with yourself and celebrate your progress, no matter how gradual. Remember that healing is a journey, and every step forward counts.

Consider Medication: In some cases, medication may be recommended as part of a comprehensive treatment plan for depression. Consult with a healthcare professional to discuss whether medication might be a helpful option for you.

SURVIVING DEPRESSION

Surviving depression is a courageous journey that requires resilience, self-compassion, and support. Here's a brief guide to navigating through depression.

Acknowledge Your Feelings: Recognize that it's okay to feel overwhelmed, and give yourself permission to experience and express your emotions.

Reach Out for Support: Lean on trusted friends, family members, or mental health professionals for guidance, understanding, and encouragement. You don't have to go through this alone.

Seek Professional Help: Consider therapy, counseling, or medication to address underlying issues and develop coping strategies tailored to your needs.

Practice Self-Care: Prioritize activities that promote physical, emotional, and mental well-being, such as exercise, healthy eating, adequate sleep, and relaxation techniques.

Challenge Negative Thoughts: Challenge self-critical and pessimistic thoughts with evidence-based reasoning, and cultivate a more compassionate and balanced perspective.

Set Small Goals: Break tasks into manageable steps and set achievable goals for yourself, celebrating each accomplishment along the way.

Engage in Meaningful Activities: Invest your time and energy in activities that bring you joy, purpose, and a sense of fulfillment.

Stay Connected: Maintain social connections and seek out supportive communities or peer groups where you can share your experiences and receive validation and encouragement.

Practice Mindfulness: Cultivate mindfulness and self-awareness through practices such as meditation, deep breathing, or yoga to stay grounded in the present moment and manage stress.

Be Patient and Persistent: Remember that recovery takes time, and setbacks are a normal part of the process. Stay committed to your self-care routine and reach out for help when needed.

Surviving depression is a journey of resilience and hope. By prioritizing self-care, seeking support, and staying resilient, you can navigate through the darkness toward a brighter future.

HOW TO AVOID DEPRESSION

Avoiding depression involves proactive steps to protect your mental well-being and build resilience. Here's a concise guide to help you stay mentally healthy:

Prioritize Self-Care: Make self-care a priority by getting regular exercise, eating a balanced diet, getting enough sleep, and avoiding harmful substances.

Stay Connected: Nurture supportive relationships with friends, family, and community members. Social support can provide comfort, encouragement, and a sense of belonging.

Manage Stress: Develop healthy coping mechanisms to manage stress, such as deep breathing, mindfulness, or meditation. Practice time management and set boundaries to reduce overwhelm.

Set Realistic Goals: Be realistic about what you can achieve and avoid putting excessive pressure on yourself. Break tasks into smaller, manageable steps and celebrate your achievements.

Engage in Meaningful Activities: Invest your time in activities that bring you joy, fulfillment, and a sense of purpose. Pursue hobbies, volunteer, or spend time in nature to boost your mood.

Seek Professional Help: If you're struggling with persistent feelings of sadness or hopelessness, don't hesitate to seek help from a mental health professional. Therapy or medication may be beneficial.

Challenge Negative Thoughts: Recognize and challenge negative thought patterns with evidence-based reasoning. Practice self-compassion and cultivate a positive mindset.

Limit Isolation: Avoid isolating yourself, even when you're feeling down. Reach out to friends or loved ones for support, or consider joining a support group where you can connect with others who understand what you're going through.

Stay Active: Keep yourself engaged in activities that stimulate your mind and body. Regular physical activity can boost your mood and energy levels.

Practice Gratitude: Cultivate an attitude of gratitude by focusing on the positive aspects of your life. Keep a gratitude journal or simply take a moment each day to reflect on the things you're thankful for.

By taking proactive steps to care for your mental health and seeking support when needed, you can reduce your risk of depression and live a fulfilling life.

NUTRITIONAL DIET TO AVOID DEPRESSION

Maintaining a balanced and nutritious diet can play a significant role in supporting mental health and reducing the risk of depression. Here are some foods that are known to be beneficial for promoting good mental well-being:

Fatty Fish: Rich in omega-3 fatty acids, fatty fish like salmon, mackerel, and sardines can help support brain health and reduce symptoms of depression.

Leafy Greens: Leafy greens such as spinach, kale, and Swiss chard are high in folate, which has been linked to a lower risk of depression.

Berries: Berries like blueberries, strawberries, and raspberries are rich in antioxidants and flavonoids, which may help protect against oxidative stress and inflammation in the brain.

Nuts and Seeds: Nuts and seeds, including almonds, walnuts, flaxseeds, and chia seeds, are good sources of healthy fats, protein, and antioxidants, all of which support brain health.

Whole Grains: Whole grains like quinoa, brown rice, oats, and barley are rich in fiber and nutrients, providing a steady release of energy and helping to stabilize mood.

Legumes: Beans, lentils, chickpeas, and other legumes are excellent sources of protein, fiber, and complex carbohydrates, which can help regulate blood sugar levels and support mood stability.

Yogurt and Fermented Foods: Yogurt, kefir, sauerkraut, and other fermented foods contain beneficial probiotics that support gut health. Emerging research suggests a link between gut health and mental well-being.

Dark Chocolate: Dark chocolate contains flavonoids, which have been shown to have mood-boosting properties. Opt for dark chocolate with a high cocoa content (70% or higher) and consume it in moderation.

Bananas: Bananas are rich in vitamins and minerals, including vitamin B6 and potassium, which play a role in neurotransmitter synthesis and mood regulation.

Tryptophan-Rich Foods: Food high in tryptophan, such as turkey, eggs, tofu, and poultry, can support serotonin production, which is important for regulating mood and promoting feelings of well-being.

In addition to incorporating these foods into your diet, it's essential to maintain a balanced and varied eating pattern, stay hydrated, and limit the consumption of processed foods, sugary snacks, and alcohol, which can negatively impact mood and overall health.

WAYS TO HEAL FROM DEPRESSION

Healing from depression is a journey that requires patience, self-compassion, and a combination of strategies. Here's a guide to help you navigate the path to healing:

Seek Professional Help: Reach out to a therapist, counselor, or psychiatrist who can provide guidance, support, and evidence-based treatment options tailored to your needs. Therapy, medication, or a combination of both may be recommended.

Build a Support System: Surround yourself with supportive friends, family members, or support groups who can offer understanding, encouragement, and a listening ear. Sharing your struggles with trusted individuals can help lighten the emotional burden.

Practice Self-Care: Prioritize self-care activities that promote physical, emotional, and mental well-being. This includes getting regular exercise, eating nutritious meals, getting enough sleep, and engaging in activities you enjoy.

Challenge Negative Thoughts: Learn to recognize and challenge negative thought patterns with cognitive-behavioral techniques. Replace self-critical thoughts with more balanced and compassionate perspectives.

Set Realistic Goals: Break tasks into smaller, manageable steps and set achievable goals for yourself. Celebrate your accomplishments, no matter how small, as each step forward is a victory.

Engage in Meaningful Activities: Invest your time and energy in activities that bring you joy, fulfillment, and a sense of purpose. Whether it's pursuing hobbies, volunteering, or spending time in nature, doing things you love can lift your spirits.

Practice Mindfulness and Relaxation: Incorporate mindfulness meditation, deep breathing exercises, or progressive muscle relaxation into your daily routine to reduce stress, increase self-awareness, and promote relaxation.

Limit Stress: Identify sources of stress in your life and take steps to minimize or manage them. Practice time management, assertiveness, and boundary-setting to protect your mental health.

Stay Connected: Maintain social connections and seek out opportunities for meaningful interactions with others. Even when you're not feeling your best, reaching out to friends or loved ones can provide comfort and support.

Be Patient and Persistent: Recovery from depression takes time, and setbacks are a normal part of the process. Be patient with yourself and acknowledge that healing is a gradual journey. Stay committed to your self-care routine and keep moving forward, one step at a time.

Remember, healing from depression is possible, and you're not alone on this journey. Don't hesitate to reach out for help when you need it, and celebrate each small victory along the way.

AVOIDING DELUSIONS

Avoiding delusions involves maintaining a clear and rational perspective on reality. Here are some strategies to help prevent delusional thinking:

Stay Grounded in Reality: Practice critical thinking and skepticism, especially when encountering information or beliefs that seem improbable or far-fetched. Verify facts and seek evidence to support your beliefs.

Seek Objective Feedback: Engage with trusted friends, family members, or mental health professionals who can provide objective feedback and perspective on your thoughts and beliefs. Listen openly to their insights and consider alternative viewpoints.

Challenge Your Assumptions: Question your own beliefs and assumptions regularly, especially those that are strongly held or emotionally charged.

Consider whether there is evidence to support them or if they may be influenced by bias or cognitive distortions.

Stay Informed: Stay informed about current events, scientific discoveries, and social issues through reputable sources. Be wary of misinformation or conspiracy theories that may promote delusional thinking.

Practice Mindfulness: Cultivate mindfulness and self-awareness through practices such as meditation, deep breathing, or journaling. Pay attention to your thoughts and emotions without judgment, and notice any patterns of irrational thinking.

Stay Connected: Maintain social connections and seek out opportunities for meaningful interactions with others. Healthy relationships can provide valuable feedback and support, helping to ground you in reality.

Limit Substance Use: Be mindful of the effects of drugs or alcohol on your perception and cognition.

Substance use can impair judgment and increase the likelihood of delusional thinking.

Seek Professional Help: If you find yourself experiencing persistent or distressing delusions, seek help from a mental health professional. Therapy, medication, or a combination of both may be recommended to address underlying issues and promote rational thinking.

Engage in Reality-Testing: When faced with doubts or uncertainties, engage in reality-testing by seeking out objective evidence or seeking the input of others. Avoid relying solely on subjective interpretations or gut feelings.

Maintain Perspective: Remember that everyone is susceptible to irrational thinking at times, and experiencing occasional doubts or uncertainties is normal. By staying vigilant and open-minded, you can reduce the risk of being swept up in delusional beliefs.

CONCLUSION

In conclusion, avoiding depression requires a multifaceted approach that encompasses various aspects of physical, emotional, and social well-being. By prioritizing self-care activities such as regular exercise, balanced nutrition, and adequate sleep, individuals can bolster their resilience against depressive symptoms. Cultivating strong social connections and seeking support from trusted friends, family members, or mental health professionals can provide crucial emotional support and validation, reducing feelings of loneliness and isolation. Additionally, challenging negative thought patterns and maintaining realistic goals can help individuals build a more positive and adaptive mindset, mitigating the risk of falling into depressive cycles. Engaging in meaningful activities that bring joy, purpose, and fulfillment can also serve as a protective factor against depression, fostering a sense of meaning and belonging.

Ultimately, staying proactive, vigilant, and compassionate towards oneself is key to avoiding depression and promoting overall mental well-being. By incorporating these strategies into daily life and seeking help when needed, individuals can empower themselves to live happier, healthier, and more fulfilling lives.

www.ingramcontent.com/pod-product-compliance
Lightning Source LLC
Chambersburg PA
CBHW061027250726
48659CB00014B/973